SHRED IT!

SCALING THE HEIGHTS

EXTREME ROCK CLIMBING

Virginia Loh-Hagan

45TH PARALLEL PRESS

Ann Arbor, Michigan

www.cherrylakepublishing.com

Content Adviser: Liv Williams, Editor, iLivExtreme

Reading Adviser: Beth Walker Gambro, MS, Ed., Reading Consultant, Yorkville, IL

Photo Credits: © Victor Guerrero Diez/Shutterstock, cover, title page; © zhukovvvlad/ Shutterstock, 5, 6; © Aflo Co. Ltd./Alamy, 7; © Victor Guerrero Diez/Shutterstock, 8; © Greg Epperson/Shutterstock, 9; © Eric Gomez T/Shutterstock, 11; Pavel Blazek, CC BY-SA 4.0 via Wikimedia Commons, 12; © Aleksandr Medyna/Shutterstock, 13; © Beatrice Pizzi/ Shutterstock, 15; © PedkoAnton/Shutterstock, 16–17; © Andrii Vandych/Shutterstock, 18–19; © 22August/Shutterstock, 20–21; Christopher Michel, CC BY-SA 4.0 via Wikimedia Commons, 22; © Greg Epperson/Shutterstock, 25; © Tribune Content Agency LLC/Alamy, 26; © Abaca Press/ Alamy, 27; © Photobac/Shutterstock, 28; © jejim/Shutterstock, 29

Library of Congress Cataloging-in-Publication Data has been filed and is available at catalog.loc.gov

Cherry Lake Press would like to acknowledge the work of the Partnership for 21st Century Learning, a Network of Battelle for Kids. Please visit Battelle for Kids online for more information.

Printed in the United States of America

Note from publisher: Websites change regularly, and their future contents are outside of our control. Supervise children when conducting any recommended online searches for extended learning opportunities.

ABOUT THE AUTHOR

Virginia Loh-Hagan is an author, university professor, former classroom teacher, and curriculum designer. In college, she jumped off a bunk bed and broke her toe. No more jumping for her. She lives in San Diego with her very tall husband and very naughty dogs.

Table of Contents

CHAPTER 1

Doing the Impossible

Extreme rock climbing is about doing the impossible. It's about **scaling**, or climbing, walls. The challenge is the climbing. It's different from **mountaineering**. Mountaineers hike up mountains. Their goal is to get to the top. Extreme rock climbers just want to climb.

Many climbers like scaling big walls. Big walls are very big rock **faces**. Faces are surfaces. They have few **holds**. Holds are rock features that climbers can grip or step on. Climbers use holds to pull themselves up. Big walls are 1,000 feet (305 meters) or higher. They are steep and **vertical**. Vertical means straight up and down.

Extreme rock climbing takes patience and focus.

Climbers often sleep on cliffs. They sleep in hanging tents. Hanging tents attach to the wall. Big wall climbing is hard work. Climbers don't waste energy. They can't panic or lose control. They have to stay relaxed. Climbers make one move at a time. They think carefully. They can't rush to the top.

SHRED IT!

Advice from the Field

If you want to be a pro climber, get used to hard work. **Brooke Raboutou** is a pro climber. She trains 4 to 6 hours each day. She does this 5 days a week. She lifts weights. She does **cardio**. This means cardiovascular exercise. It strengthens your heart. She also does exercises to increase her mental strength. This involves visualization and breathwork. Raboutou does **hangboarding**, too. This is a type of strength training. People hang from a board with different holds. They practice lifting themselves up. It improves their grip strength. Raboutou also works on her speed and endurance. She placed fifth in the 2020 Olympic Games. She kept training. She won a silver medal at the 2024 Olympics. In 2025, she made history. She climbed Excalibur. She was the first woman ever to climb something that difficult. Her advice to other athletes? "Have fun while you are doing it. These days there are a lot of hard working athletes, which is so important, but sometimes take the time to just enjoy your sport for your sport."

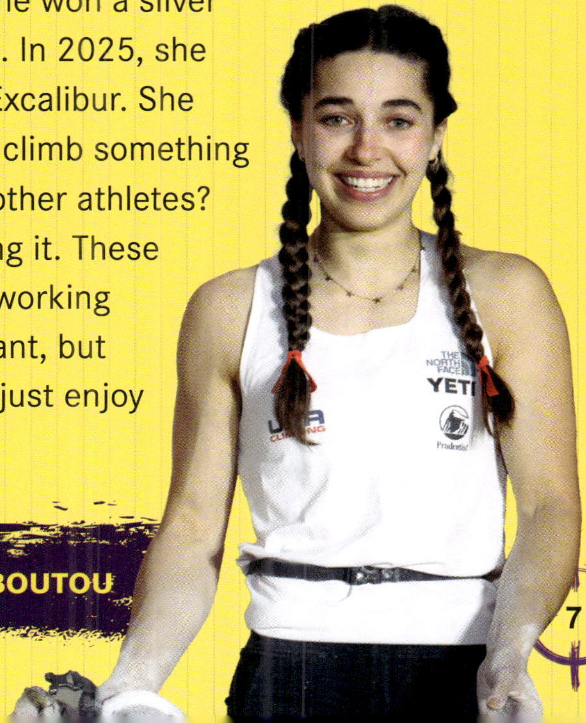

BROOKE RABOUTOU

Rock climbing has many benefits. Climbing builds muscle. It boosts brainpower. It builds problem-solving skills. Climbers must figure out how to climb. And they have fun while doing it. That's what extreme rock climbing is all about.

How do climbers stay calm in scary situations? They take deep breaths. They visualize their goals. They try to relax their bodies. Being mentally prepared for a climb is important. Extreme rock climbers wouldn't make it to the top otherwise.

Teams of climbers often work together to ensure safe climbs.

CHAPTER 2

To Know or Not to Know...

Climbers like completing **routes** on their first try. Routes are climbing paths. Climbers have different ways to do this.

Flash climbing is when climbers receive some beta before the climb. Beta is information. Climbers help each other. They share good holds. They share moves.

This helps climbers be successful on their first try. Onsight climbing is when climbers have no beta. Climbers try to complete a climb on the first try without any help. They stand on the ground. They look up. They figure out routes. They look for holds. Onsight climbing is hard.

Some climbers fail to complete a climb by onsight or flash. This does not have to stop them. They may redpoint the climb instead.

In redpoint climbing, climbers free-climb a route they have attempted before. They practice and learn about the route. They keep trying until they succeed.

Many climbers suggest being open to new ideas. Whether they get it the first time or not, climbers need to make changes as they climb.

One of the hardest climbing routes in the world is called *Silence*. It is in Flatanger, Norway. Climber Adam Ondra successfully climbed in 2017. He had to redpoint the climb. It took him 7 visits and more than 40 days of climbing to reach his goal. He is one of the world's best climbers.

EXTREME ROCK CLIMBING:

Know the Lingo

Airtime: long fall

Barndoor: a climber who is holding on by only his left or right hand and foot—he swings out from the wall like a door

Belay: to protect a roped climber from falling by passing the rope through a belay device

Beta: information about a route that helps climbers

Carabiners: metal rings used to guide a climber's safety rope

Deck: the ground

Dyno: jump or leap or lunge

Edging: using the edge of a shoe on a foothold

Greasy: slippery

Gripped: tired or afraid

Pitch: section of a cliff that is climbed between two belay points

Pumped: feeling in the forearms when muscles lose strength after a hard climb

Rappel: descend a rock face by sliding down a rope

Rest: big handholds and footholds that let the climber relax

Send: to cleanly complete a route (short for ascend)

Smearing: when there is no foothold, using the sole of a shoe on the wall

Whip: end of a long fall

CARABINERS

CHAPTER 3

There's a Way Up for Every Climber!

Every climb is different. Every climb has risks. Some climbers take it to the extreme. They challenge themselves. They test their skills. They keep reaching for the top.

FREE CLIMBING

Free climbing is a test of strength. It is a test of skill. Climbers are attached to ropes for safety. But a successful free climb doesn't put weight on them. Climbers cannot **hang**. That is when the ropes hold a climber up. If a free climber gets **aid**, or help from the ropes, they did not succeed.

FREE SOLO
CLIMBING

Free solo climbing is dangerous. These climbers don't use ropes or any gear. They only use shoes and a chalk bag. They must be skilled and strong. They must be careful. Nothing protects them but themselves.

ES PONTAS, SPAIN

DEEP WATER SOLO CLIMBING

Deep water soloing uses the ocean as a safety net. Climbers climb sea cliffs at high tide. If climbers fall, the water protects them. Small boats pick them up. The water can also be dangerous. Climbers can drown.

BIG WALL CLIMBING

Big wall climbing takes time. It takes planning. Climbers scale giant cliffs and rock faces. A big wall is hundreds or thousands of feet or meters high. It takes more than a day to climb. Climbers must carry everything they need.

Climbers sleep on the wall. They **anchor** themselves and their gear. Anchor means attach to the climbing surface. This keeps them safe. The most famous big wall is El Capitan. It is in Yosemite National Park in California. It is 3,000 feet (914 m) tall.

THE NORTH FACE
THE NORTH FACE

SHRED IT! SPOTLIGHT: Alex Honnold

Alex Honnold is a free solo climber. He had a dream. He wanted to free solo El Capitan. El Capitan means "the captain" in Spanish. Honnold worked hard. He trained. He studied the rock face. He completed his climb in 2017. He did it in 3 hours and 56 minutes. This had never been done before! In an interview with *National Geographic* following his climb, he was overjoyed. He said, "Honestly, I think this is the most satisfied I've ever been. It was exactly what I hoped for. I felt so good. It went pretty much perfectly." The documentary *Free Solo* shows his journey to achieve this dream. Honnold didn't stop there. In 2024, Honnold set the speed record on El Capitan's Salathé Wall route. The previous record was over 20 hours. Honnold did it in just over 11 hours.

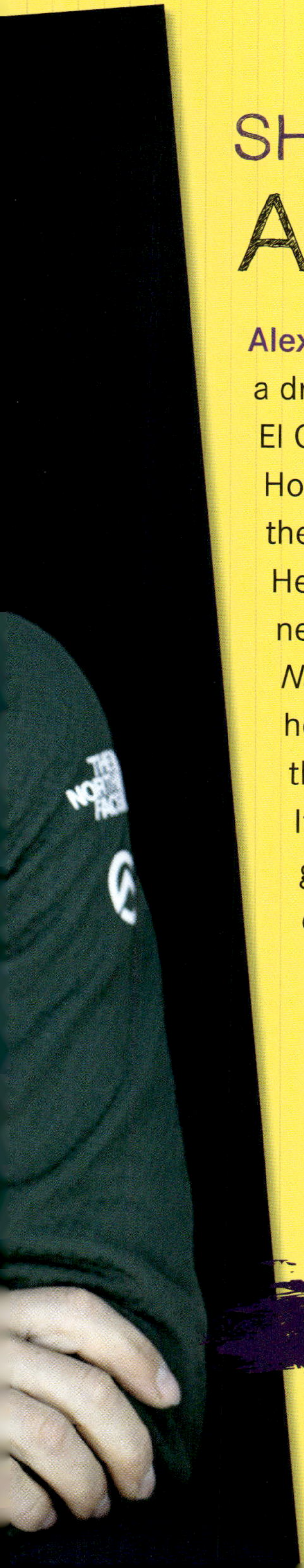

ALEX HONNOLD

CHAPTER 4

Keep Shredding!

Extreme rock climbing is dangerous. Loose rocks are dangerous. Sudden weather changes are dangerous. Climbers can fall. They can break body parts. Falling rocks can hit them. Climbers need to be smart. They use their skills. They are creative.

But sometimes, the unexpected still happens.

Patience and endurance are the keys to climbing success.

Tommy Caldwell is a big wall climber. He free-climbed The Nose on El Capitan. This big wall route is 2,900 feet (884 m) tall. The unstoppable Caldwell did it in less than 12 hours.

Not even war stops Caldwell. In 2000, he and 3 friends climbed cliffs in Kyrgyzstan. This country is in central Asia. A war was taking place there between the government and **rebels**. Rebels are people who take action against a government.

Caldwell and his friends camped out. They used **ledges**, which are flat surfaces that jut out from the rock face. They used tents. They were hundreds of feet in the air.

They heard gunshots. They were captured by rebels. They were prisoners for 6 days. One day, they were alone with a rebel. Caldwell pushed the rebel over the edge. Caldwell and his friends used their climbing skills to escape. They climbed for several miles. Caldwell later learned that the rebel survived the fall.

Extreme rock climbing challenges both body and mind.

Tristan Chen is another active member of the extreme climbing community. He loves getting out on a wall in nature and puzzling through a climb. But in 2022, he was diagnosed with **leukemia**. This type of cancer affects a person's blood. Chen had to go through months of treatment. Afterward, he could barely do 2 pull-ups. But he got back into climbing. This helped him recover.

Extreme rock climbers don't let anything get in their way.

SHRED IT!

When Extreme Is Too Extreme!

Climbers are always trying to do something no one else has. In 2017, Leah Pappajohn and Jonathan Fleury did just that. They climbed El Capitan naked! They were the first people to do this. They both got their personal best times for the climb. Leah felt like climbing nude was empowering. She also thought it was funny. Overall, it was a great experience, except for the sunburn.

EL CAPITAN

DID YOU KNOW?

- Climbers don't have bathrooms available. They have to relieve themselves in nature. They stay away from plants, climbing routes, streams, and trails. They get rid of their own waste. They carry plastic bags for used toilet paper. While big wall climbing, climbers have to do their business. They pee in the air. They use toilet sacks, called "wag bags," when they have to poop. They save these to trash later. Or they send the bags to helpers on the ground.

- Some climbers play a game called Add On. One climber does a route. The next climber repeats the route and adds a move. This is repeated until they get bored or tired.

- Rock climbers have nicknames. They are called rock hounds, rock jocks, or wall rats.

- Climbers wear shoes that are a size or two smaller than their normal shoes. They also don't wear socks. They want to have a tight fit. They want to feel the rock.

CONSIDER THIS!

TAKE A POSITION! Some climbers think people should not free solo. They think it's too dangerous. Some believe it is **unethical**. This means not morally right. What if other people copy a free solo climber, and then get injured or die? What danger will teams that rescue fallen climbers face? What do you think? Should free soloing be outlawed? Argue your point with reasons and evidence.

SAY WHAT? Extreme rock climbers use many of the same skills as mountaineers. Mountaineers climb to explore. But rock climbers are also different from mountaineers. Learn more about mountaineering. Explain the differences and similarities between the 2 sports.

THINK ABOUT IT! Rock climbing has a grading system. This system describes the difficulty and danger of climbing the route. There are 5 classes. Class 1 describes easy hikes. Class 5 is where a fall may result in death. Compare this grading system to your grading system at school. Why do we need grades?

SEE A DIFFERENT SIDE! The U.S. Forest Service bans some climbing gear. Climbing gear could become a permanent part of the rock formation. **Bouldering** causes concerns as well. This type of rock climbing is done without ropes or harnesses. It is on lower walls. Officials worry about destroying nature. Many climbers believe in "leave no trace" and "minimal impact." This means they leave nature as they found it. How can rock climbing be harmful to nature?

LEARN MORE

BOOKS

Eberth, Krissy and Kristin Eberth. *Curious About Rock Climbing.* Mankato, MN: Amicus Learning, 2024.

Miller, Tracey. *Free Solo Climbing.* Mankato, MN: Creative Education, 2025.

WEBSITES

With an adult, explore more online with these suggested searches.

American Alpine Club | Stories

International Climbing and Mountaineering Federation

GLOSSARY

aid (AYD) help; or the use of equipment in climbing to assist upward movement

anchor (ANK-uhr) to securely attach to a climbing surface to protect from falls

bouldering (BOHL-dur-ing) a form of rock climbing without harnesses or ropes on shorter walls

cardio (KAR-dee-oh) short for cardiovascular exercise, which strengthens the heart

faces (FA-sez) rock surfaces

hang (HANG) to dangle from a rope or hold without touching the wall

hangboarding (HANG-bord-ing) strength-training exercise where people hang from a board with different holds to increase grip strength

holds (HOHLDZ) cracks, ledges, and other features climbers use

ledges (LEH-juhz) rock shelves on the mountain walls

leukemia (loo-KEE-mee-uh) a type of blood cancer

mountaineering (mown-tuh-NEER-ing) a sport in which people hike up mountains

rebels (REH-buhlz) people who go against the government in charge

routes (ROWTS) climbing paths

scaling (SKAY-ling) climbing a steep wall

unethical (un-ETH-ih-kuhl) not morally right

vertical (VER-tih-kuhl) straight up

INDEX